Life in the Amazon Rain Forest

by Ronald Scheibel

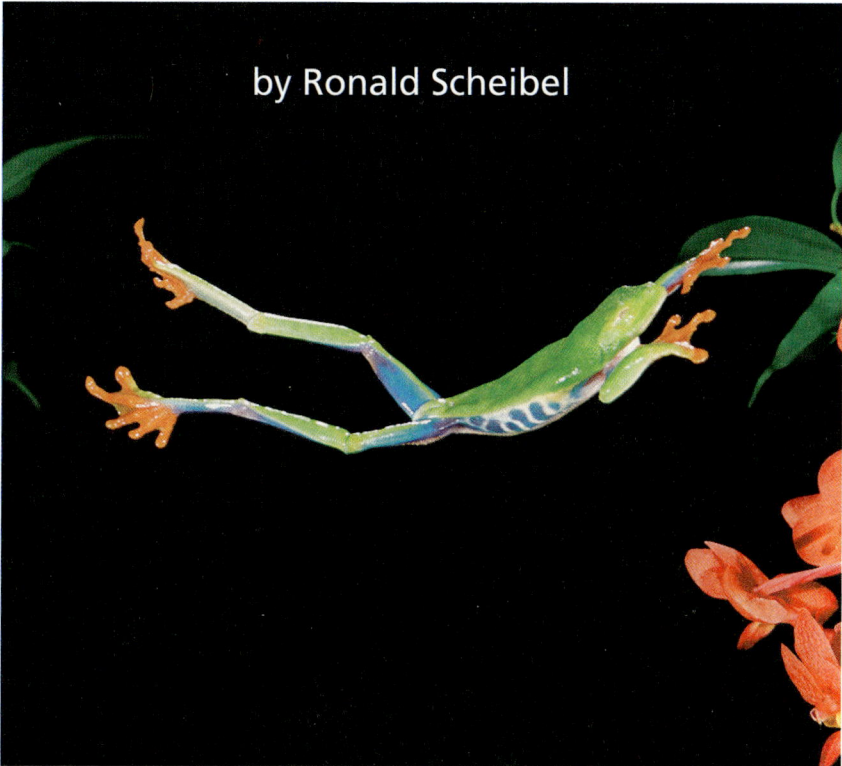

PEARSON

Glenview, Illinois • Boston, Massachusetts • Chandler, Arizona
Upper Saddle River, New Jersey

Life in the Amazon Rain Forest

Think of a building where each floor, or level, is used for something different. The ground floor might be a store. The second floor might be an office. The top floors might be apartments.

The Amazon rain forest also has four levels. Each level is different from the others. The four levels are:

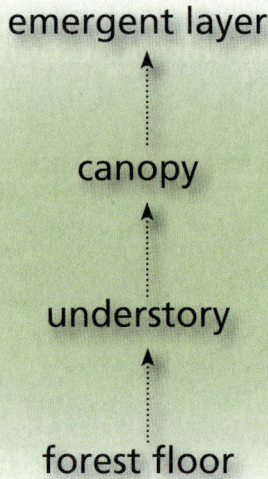

emergent layer

↑

canopy

↑

understory

↑

forest floor

Let's take a trip to the top of the rain forest habitat. Hundreds of insects and animals live at each level. We will catch glimpses of a few!

---

habitat: place where a plant or animal lives

Before We Climb

Before we climb up to the treetops, let's look around.

First, everything is wet. In the Amazon, most of the rain falls in the afternoon. More than half of all fresh water on Earth is in the Amazon River system.

Also, it is dark. Huge trees reach more than 150 feet tall. Their thick branches block the sunlight all day long. Most of these trees spread out like fans near the ground. The soil is shallow, so the trees need wide roots to get a good "foothold." These are called buttress roots.

---

shallow: not deep
buttress roots: wide roots that spread out all around the base of tall rain forest trees

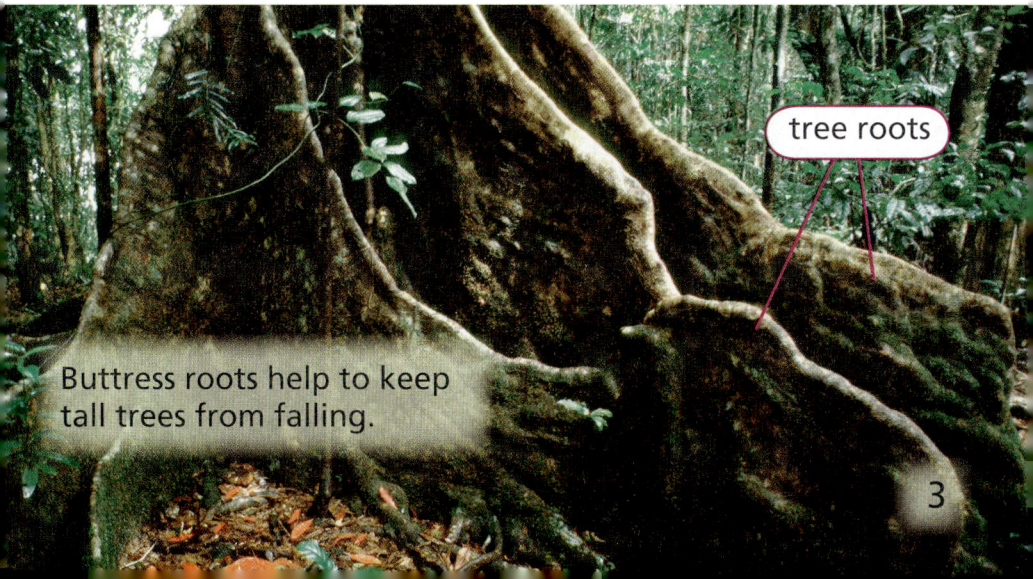

tree roots

Buttress roots help to keep tall trees from falling.

The Forest Floor

Down on the ground, insects buzz, birds call, and monkeys howl. As many as 43 <mark>species</mark> of ants crawl up and down on a single tree.

One species of ant, the leafcutter ant, lives in large colonies of up to seven million! Their underground nests can be as large as your classroom. These ants clear large areas. They carry pieces of leaves back to their nest. But they don't eat the leaves. They use the leaves to help grow a <mark>fungus</mark>. This fungus is food for the ants. The leafcutter ants are like farmers, growing the food they need.

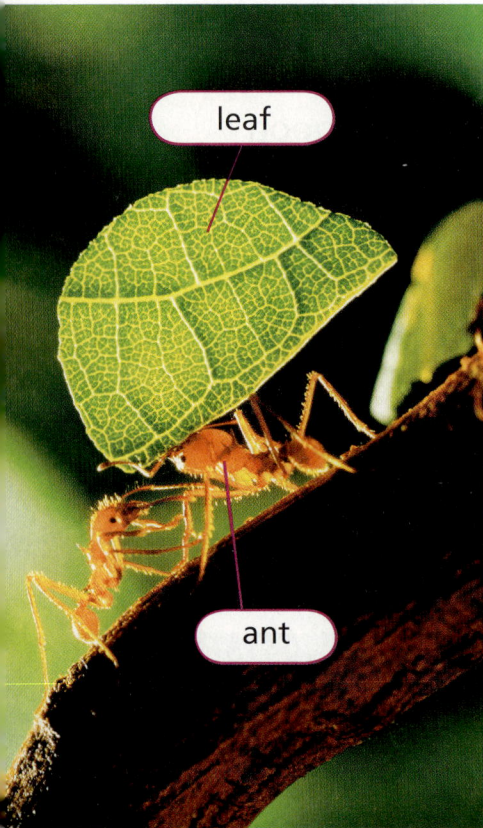

leaf

ant

A leafcutter ant
hard at work

---

species: a category
fungus: a type of living thing that absorbs food

The Understory

Let's move up to the understory. There is plenty of room between the large tree trunks for smaller trees, ferns, vines, and palms. Many plants cling to the surface of tree trunks and have no roots in the ground.

Giant, poisonous tarantula spiders live in the understory. They can be as large as 10 inches across. They hunt small frogs, lizards, and birds.

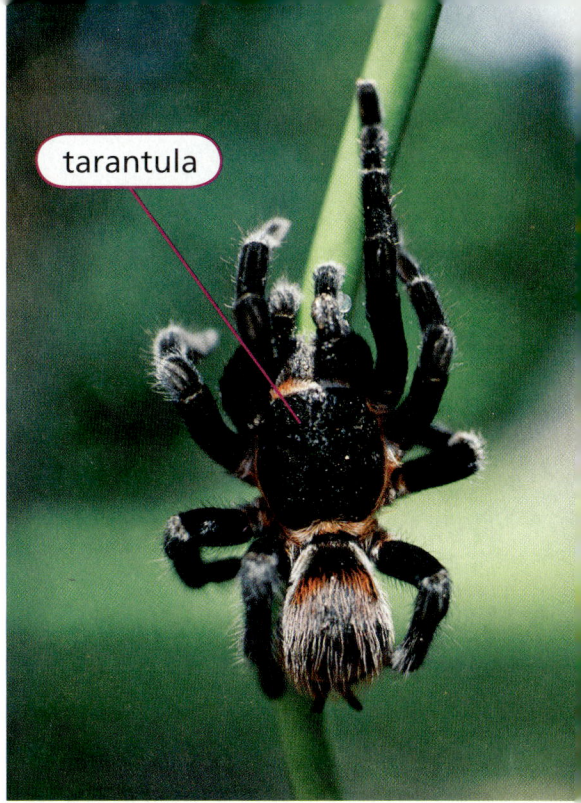

tarantula

The tarantula feeds on frogs, lizards, and birds.

You might also see bats at this level. We think of bats as blind insect eaters. But in the Amazon, there are bats that can see. They go from flower to flower, sipping nectar and carrying pollen. This is good for the bats and for the flowers.

---

understory: the level just above the ground, where bushes and small trees live

opossum

Monkeys and opossums sleep at different times, so they can share a home.

The Canopy

Don't look down! Now we're more than 100 feet above the ground! This is the canopy, where the tree branches block out sunlight. There are so many branches, monkeys can leap from tree to tree.

The canopy is the busiest level in the rain forest. Here you might see a colorful toucan (bird) eating fruit or a hairy sloth (mammal) hanging from a branch.

The canopy is so crowded that some animals share their homes. During the day, the nocturnal opossum sleeps in a hole in a tree. At night, a monkey sleeps in the same hole while the opossum finds food outside of it.

nocturnal: active at night and sleeping during the day

The Emergent Layer

Finally, we're at the <mark>emergent layer</mark>. What a great view! Trees need to grow at least 130 feet tall to stick out above the canopy.

Here you might see a tree frog using its webbed hands and feet to glide up to 40 feet. Here, you can see the sun and feel a breeze. Here, it is also drier than at any other level.

This layer is less crowded than the canopy, but still, more than 1,800 species of birds and 250 species of mammals live here. You will see some surprising animals, including iguanas and tiny mouse opossums.

This afternoon, the rain clouds are forming. Let's head home and tell everyone about the amazing world in the Amazon rain forest!

---

emergent layer: the top rain forest level, where only a few trees grow above the canopy

frog

The tree frog glides with its webbed hands and feet.

The Four-Level Rain Forest

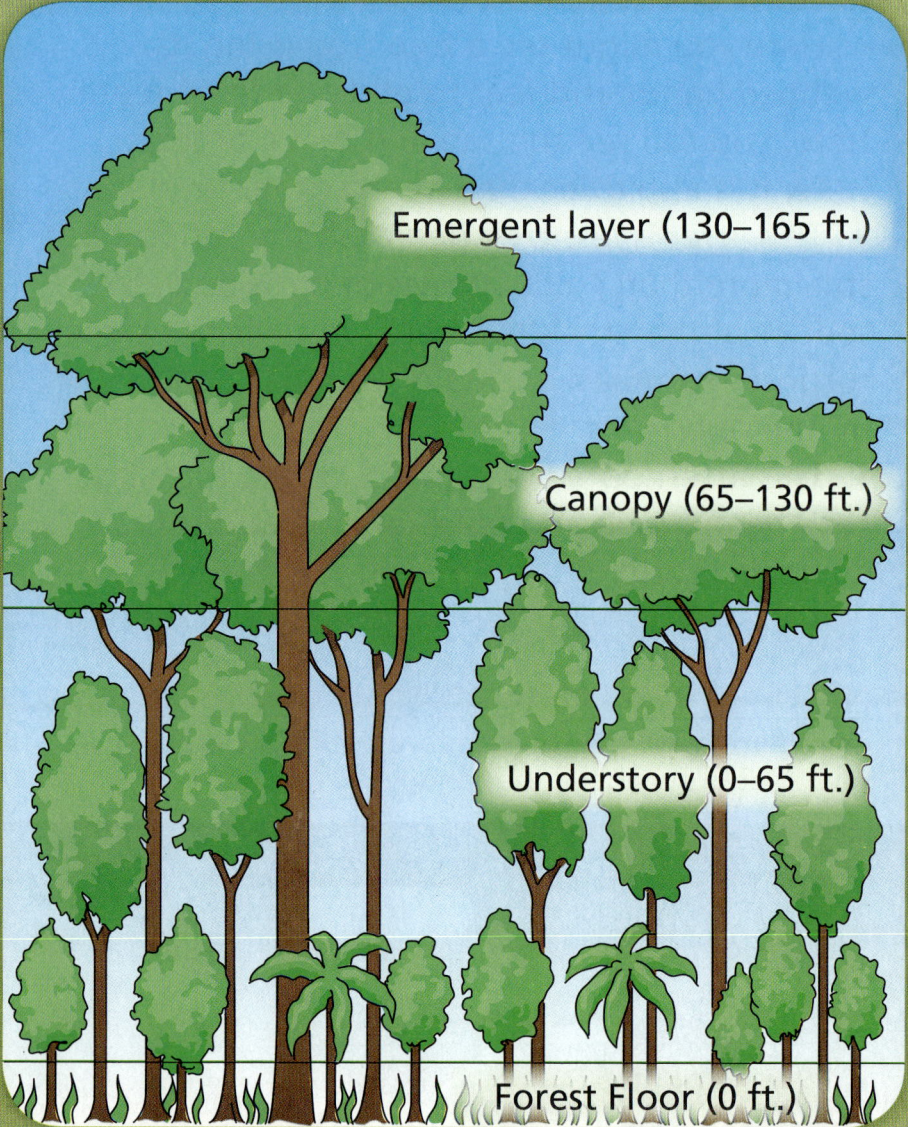

Emergent layer (130–165 ft.)

Canopy (65–130 ft.)

Understory (0–65 ft.)

Forest Floor (0 ft.)